Cornfed, Countrified, and Consecrated

musings and inspirations
from a life well-lived

Dorothy Dale

CORNFED, COUNTRIFIED, AND CONSECRATED

MUSINGS AND INSPIRATIONS FROM A LIFE WELL-LIVED

By Dorothy Dale

Published by DMD Productions

Printed in the United States of America

First Printing, 2012

ISBN 978-0615682785

Book and Cover Design by DJ Westerfield

TABLE OF CONTENTS

DEDICATION

First, I thank the Lord Who gave me some talent and Who continually forms thoughts in my mind which I just have to write down.

A special thank you to friends through the years who have encouraged me to put my poems in a book: to the Plateau Writers and the Write Touch Inspirational Writers groups who inspired me to keep on writing: and to Rev. Charles Christopher whose sermons have given me many ideas for poems and essays.

And lastly, to DJ Westerfield without whose expertise this book would not have been possible.

PREFACE

I grew up on a farm in southwest Michigan. We had no electricity, no running water, and an "outhouse" in the back yard. We got electricity the year I graduated from high school. The beauty of growing up in a rural area in the 1940s was that we didn't know any other way of life. With little communication, we thought everyone lived just the way we did.

I have become used to modern conveniences. I really wouldn't want to go back to the "good old days". But if some tragic disaster should happen, and I had to live off the land, I know that I could survive.

I started writing poems at the age of 15 as a way of expressing my deepest feelings, which were (and still are) difficult for me to share orally.

The poems and stories here are all pieces of my life. They chronicle my thoughts and lessons learned from the time I was growing up country, through love's joys and agonies, surviving the death of a loving husband, to a life of service to God. I know now that through it all God was watching over me even though, for many years, I was unaware of His care.

Dorothy Dale

GROWING UP COUNTRY

LOVELY DANGER: My very first vivid memory. Every detail is etched forever on my mind.

MAKING DO: We never threw anything away. We were recycling long before anyone had heard the word. Everything could be repurposed.

COUNTRY GIRL: This is the way I felt about my life in the country at age 15. I still am a country girl at heart.

MOMMA AND THE COW: One of my favorite memories. We nearly had a lot of beef to eat that winter.

HAVE YOU EVER: I have always been a nature lover. I feel closest to God while communing with "Mother Nature".

RUSTY'S GIFT: This experience drastically changed my outlook on life. I still remember every moment I spent with this special animal.

UNEXPLAINED: This is the first time that I was aware that there had to be some mysterious power (God? Guardian Angel?) which was watching over me.

SPRING STORM: A proof of the unpredictability of the weather in Michigan's "Snow Belt". I never want to be this cold again!

MY MICHIGAN: This is the way I saw Michigan at the time. But, since making Tennessee my home in 1989, I tell people I can't help where I was born.

LOVELY DANGER

My very first memory is of an incident on a summer day when I was about 2 years old. I was busy learning about the world around me: exploring, touching, and moving on to new adventures. Everything interested me and I had not yet learned to be cautious--that there were unknown dangers in my universe.

We lived in a small ram-shackled house in the country. The pitcher pump stood just outside the kitchen door. About 100 feet away, at the edge of the wooded hill sloping down to the Black River, was our very own two-seater out house. We did have a basement (better known as a cellar). The cellar stairway was at the side of the house near the kitchen door. It was covered with a crude home-made door which rested on a row of cement blocks along one side, and was attached to the house with two large iron hinges on the other side.

We owned--or were owned by--a huge black and white dog named Stub. He was mostly German Shepherd, with just enough bull-dog to give him a formidable looking chest, and a little collie for loyalty. He had appointed himself the sole guardian and care-taker of my 6-month old sister and me.

On this particular day, we had just come home from our monthly trip into town to the grocery store. I toddled behind my mother as she carried my sister in one arm and a bag of groceries in the other. As she stepped through the kitchen door and set the grocery bag on the table, my attention strayed to a movement near the cellar door.

What an interesting sight! "Pretty, pretty," I said as I bent to touch the multi-colored creature coiled inside one of the cement blocks. Suddenly, Stub was beside me, growling and pushing me sideways with his shoulder.

My mother turned to see what the commotion was just as I shoved the dog aside and reached again to pet my lovely new-found toy. "Pretty, pretty," I repeated.

My mother shocked me when she yelled. I couldn't understand why she grabbed the hoe that leaned in a nearby corner and began beating my pretty new friend as I screamed in anger. How could she do this?

Only after it was over did momma give me my first lesson in nature studies: You just don't pet a five-foot long rattle snake!

MAKING DO

Before the days of recycling and garage sales, our family made use of everything--not only our own well-worn items, but also those of our friends and neighbors.

I don't remember why people started giving us boxes of used clothing, but I vividly recall how we made use of them.

After washing everything in our old Maytag, my mother, sister, and I laid claim to all wearable clothes that fit us. The remaining garments were a treasure-trove of fabrics we used for three purposes: crocheted rugs, hooked rugs, and quilts.

We tore the cloth into 1" wide strips for the rugs. Heavy material such as wool and corduroy went to Grandma for her intricately beautiful hooked rugs made on a backing of burlap bags. These she sold for extra "pin money".

My sister and I crocheted the thinner strips into huge round or oval throw rugs to warm the floors of our old farm house during the cold Michigan winters. Our hooks were gigantic--carved from old broom handles. I don't know when I learned to crochet. It was just something we did. A far cry from the lacy designs I make today.

Fine fabrics such as velvet or silk were set aside to be used in "Crazy Quilts". I still have the velvet one Grandma gave me. The colorful irregular patches outlined in yellow feather stitching remind me of another time--full of hard work and "making do".

COUNTRY GIRL

I guess I'm just a country girl--
I've never lived in town--
But I wouldn't trade this country life
For all the money 'round.

Come morning when the sun comes up
I like to be awake
To see the changing of the clouds--
The colors that they take.

Where else but in the country, now,
Can someone come to call
Without the whole wide countryside
Knowing who was there and all?

That's why I like this country life.
I guess I'll always be
The one who'll fight for country ways--
For nature you can see.

MOMMA AND THE COW

My mother was a loving, hard-working woman who unobtrusively carried on her duties raising two daughters and caring for my father and his parents. My grandmother, who was ill, demanded a lot of care. In her "spare" time, Momma worked in the fields helping to maintain our 80 acre farm.

During all of this time, I don't recall ever seeing Momma show much emotion. Outbursts of anger or frustration just weren't allowed in our household--except by Daddy or his mother. Momma kept all of her feelings closely guarded until one fateful day when the cow got out of the pasture and visited us at the house.

Momma had a Christmas Cactus among her collection of house plants. Oh, what a glorious specimen it was! It had belonged to my grandmother and to her mother before that. Over the years it had outgrown a succession of containers until it made its home in a galvanized wash tub. The cactus was so big that it showered down over the sides of the tub. It started blooming by Thanksgiving each year and continued to be covered by a breathtaking crimson cascade until the following Easter.

During most of the year, it occupied a place of honor in the bay window of our living room. But my father and grandfather lugged it outside to rest on an old table in front of that window during the warmest summer months.

One bright summer day, Momma glanced out the bay window, screamed, and headed for the door. There, calmly gazing in the window was our old milk cow, a long strand of Christmas Cactus dangling from each side of her mouth. The washtub was empty except for a few green spikes.

Beside the side door to the porch stood two items: a broom and my father's loaded shotgun. As Momma rounded the corner and flew out the door, her hand landed on one of these and she dragged it with her out into the yard. Luckily for the cow, it was the broom.

Then ensued the funniest--and saddest--few minutes I recall from my childhood. Momma chased that cow around the house, around the granary, across the garden, and back around the house several times. The cow was running for her life, tail in the air, cowbell clapping, bellowing in terror. Momma was one step behind, screaming unintelligibly at the top of her lungs, tears streaming down her cheeks, and swinging that broom with every ounce of strength she had--and her aim was infallible.

The cow finally returned to where she had squeezed through the fence and scurried back to safety, turning around to gaze at this disheveled banshee that had been chasing her.

Momma returned to the house, still crying, picked up the broken remnants of the cactus, threw them in the garbage, then went about her duties. No one ever talked about her outburst later on. But my feelings are a mixture of heartache and hilarity every time I recall that day.

Oh, yes, the cactus has recovered. The few remaining stubs continued to sprout new growth, and now, some 60 years later, it is almost as big as it was when the cow decided to have lunch.

HAVE YOU EVER

Have you ever sat beside a stream
Underneath the towering trees,
And listened to it sing its song
Rippled briskly by the breeze?

Have you ever looked across a lake
When the sun was sinking low,
Seeing how the sky was making
All the colors gently glow?

Have you ever pondered on a plain
While watching bees go buzzing by,
Wondering who made mountains misty
And what makes up the bright blue sky?

How I love to look for wonders!
All of us--God gave us these;
Oh, if only I could help Him
All the people now to please.

RUSTY'S GIFT

"You don't understand me--nobody understands me! And you don't care!" I slammed the door behind me and stumbled along the road to catch the high school bus, angry tears streaming down my cheeks.

Twelve years old, and physically developed beyond my years, I was at that awful age when I was no longer a child, but not yet a woman. Overweight, and the youngest person in the freshman class, I wanted desperately to be part of the crowd. But, because of my age, my parents did not allow me to attend the parties that my older classmates regularly held. We argued about it frequently.

That day in school was much the same all the others. It seemed like I was invisible. I sat in class, walked down the hallways, and worked in the lunchroom, but no one seemed to know that I was there. They talked at me, but not to me.

As I stepped off the bus that night, I had no idea that God was about to provide me with a friend.

The last mile of gravel read that led in from the blacktop was always a lonely walk for me. After the bus dropped me off at the corner, I would not see another human being until I got home. We were the only family living on the back country road at the time. I was so overwhelmed by self-pitying and negative thoughts that I didn't enjoy the quiet and peaceful winter scene around me.

I don't know how long the fox had watched me. When I first noticed her, she was crouched in the snow behind a bramble bush, her wary eyes following my every move. She probably thought she was hidden from sight, and I certainly hadn't expected to see her there. I'm not sure who was the most surprised when our eyes met.

I spoke to her softly, fully expecting her to run. But she watched me curiously and quivered. I don't remember what I said to her, but I kept my voice calm and soft so I wouldn't frighten her. Her ears twitched as I spoke.

After a few minutes of one-sided conversation, I hurried on home so as not to be late in starting my farm chores. I loved all animals, and I was pleased that this wild thing had not been afraid of me. Perhaps she had sensed my loneliness--maybe she was lonely, too. But here was a being that was actually listening to me. I didn't think anybody listened to me anymore--or cared about my feelings.

The next day I was astonished to find the fox waiting for me. She wasn't hiding now. She sat up tall and looked straight at me. I spoke to her again and moved one step closer to her. She didn't move. One more cautious step. This time she retreated slightly. So I kept on talking and backed away from her, down the road toward home. She was following me! She stayed across the ditch and about ten feet behind, and I talked to her as we walked. About half way down the road she silently disappeared into the brush.

She met me every day after that. Soon she was following just a nose-length behind me. I told her everything: the frustrations, the agony, the desires--all the secret thoughts that I was sure no one else would care about. I called her Rusty. She was my soul mate, my confidant, my only true friend. But she wouldn't allow me to touch her.

All that long winter she walked me half way home each day after school, meeting and leaving me at the same spots each time. Eventually she started to walk beside me, just out of reach of my finger tips.

The last fluffy snow of the season was on the ground. Rusty and I were about midway through our daily walk when she suddenly froze in her tracks. Instinctively, I stopped and watched her. Her ears twitched. Her eyes glowed. Like a slingshot, she catapulted through the air and dove headfirst into a snow bank across the ditch. When she came up, she had a rabbit in her jaws. It amazed me how fast she had moved. I had the feeling that I was witnessing an act of nature that very few humans had ever observed.

Rusty brought the still-quivering rabbit to me and laid it at my feet. As she sat down, I moved on, thinking that she would pick it up and eat it. But she brought it to me again and presented it in the same manner. She definitely intended for me to have it. As I tried to swallow the lump in my throat, I realized that she was giving me a gift--the only way she could.

I knelt to touch the still warm body in the snow, debating on what I should do. Then Rusty came to me. For the first time, she allowed me to touch her. I buried my face in her thick fur and sobbed. She stood patiently until the feeling passed, then pushed the dead rabbit closer to me with her nose. Her message was clear, so I picked it up and carried it home.

Tears came again as I tried to explain to my parents where the rabbit came from. And they listened. For the first time ever, it seemed, they heard what I had to say. We talked long into the night, and I slept with the knowledge that they really did care.

I never saw Rusty after that. Maybe the lengthening days had awakened within her the need for her own kind, and the rabbit was her farewell gift to me. My heart ached with her loss, but my newly found friendship with my parents eased the pain. Rusty's job was finished.

That spring a whole new world opened up to me. Following Rusty's example, I brought a handful of flowers to my mother. I ironed my father's shirts without grousing. I hoed the garden for my grandfather. I brought dinner, with a smile, to my bed-ridden grandmother.

As my attitude toward those around me changed, people became friendlier. I knew that an animal loved me enough to give of herself to me. I knew now that my parents loved me. Since I felt that I was loved, I was free to pass that feeling on to others. I found that love is a sharing thing. And I learned to recognize and accept graciously the small caring acts and words I had formerly overlooked.

There are times, even now, when I'm driving down the road to the old homestead that the thrill of Rusty's gift returns to me. She was my friend; she never broke a confidence. She never passed the secrets I told her on to others. She helped me through a very difficult time in my life by just being there to listen.

My goal now is to "be there" for others who may need a listening ear, a shoulder to cry on, a small act of caring. It's my way of passing on a bit of God's love.

Rusty, your gift is remembered.

UNEXPLAINED

The summer after I turned 15, I worked as a waitress at Sunnybrook Farm, a resort near where I lived, a few miles from South Haven, Michigan.

We served the meals family style. One of my duties was to help clean up the dining room and kitchen after the guests were done.

One afternoon, after we had finished our cleaning detail, the waitresses and bus boys were standing around in the spacious kitchen chatting with the cooks. We had developed some close friendships that summer, and often talked for awhile before leaving for the day.

As I stood there, I felt a sharp jolt from behind, as if someone had fallen against me. To regain my balance, I took a step forward and a little to my left.

A split second later, a large object hit the floor right where I had been standing. The kitchen vent fan had somehow torn apart. The electric motor, which weighed at least 40 pounds, had crashed into the floor, doing extensive damage. Had I still been in that spot, I would surely have been badly injured--if not killed.

Everyone gathered around me, making sure that I was not hurt, and commenting on how lucky it was that I had decided to move at that precise time.

When I told them that someone had shoved me, they were puzzled. There had been no one else in the kitchen--no one behind me--no one who could have pushed me out of harm's way.

But "someone" did.

Psalm 91:9-13

SPRING STORM

Sunday, April 16, 1961, started out as a lovely spring day in southwest Michigan. The sun was shining, the early wildflowers and fruit trees were in bloom, and a clear sky promised a warm day. By ten a.m. the temperature climbed to 70 degrees.

"It's a beautiful day for a drive. Would you like to go down to Benton Harbor and have lunch with my cousins?" Frank asked as I opened the door to let him in. "They called last night to invite us. They'd like to meet you."

I had met Frank a few weeks earlier through mutual friends. We had spent quite a bit of time together getting acquainted. My husband had deserted me and our son, Danny, several months before. I was spending all of my time working and caring for Danny, who was 17 months old. It felt good to have a new friend.

"Sure," I said, "It sounds like fun. I need to get away for a while."

I packed up a few diapers, a change of clothes, and a jar of Gerbers peaches for Danny. He normally ate whatever we did, but just in case.......

Our drive to Benton Harbor took the usual 30 minutes in the bright sunshine. Frank's cousins welcomed us warmly, and we had a bountiful dinner around their huge oak dinner table. Just as we were starting to clear the dishes away, someone noticed that it had started snowing--hard!

By one o'clock about 6 inches of snow covered the ground and we decided to start home. At two o'clock the car radio announced that the State Police were closing all roads. No one was to venture out. But we were already out on U.S. 31 headed toward home--very slowly.

Huge fluffy wet snow flakes filled the air. The wipers could barely clear the windshield. Visibility was about 20 feet. As we crept along, trying to stay on the now invisible road, I fed Danny the jar of peaches, changed his last diaper, and put him down in the back seat for a nap.

By five o'clock our half-hour drive had lasted four hours and we were only half way home. I thought how lucky it was that we had used my car, which I had filled with gas the day before, instead of Frank's, which was nearly empty. I began to worry, however. After dark we would have even more difficulty seeing the road.

Danny woke from his nap. There was no more food, no dry diapers, and no toys. For a hungry, wet, bored little boy this was intolerable.

At nine o'clock we finally reached the corner of Phoenix Road and 66th Street. By taking this gravel road the 1 mile over to Baseline Road, we would be within ¼ mile of my house. We stopped at the corner and debated. The wind had picked up. Snow was still falling, and the narrow road could be drifted full. We decided to try it rather than go the extra mile to the next crossroad, which was paved, and then have to back-track to my house. Bad decision.

As we crept around the corner, the wind blew a white-out of snow across the road. We ended up in the ditch. Luckily, the people who lived in the farmhouse on the corner were friends of my parents. Frank went to the door, introduced himself, and asked if he could pull us out with his tractor. He agreed, bundled up, got the tractor out of the barn, hooked onto the rear bumper--and pulled it off with the first tug. After re-attaching the chain to a sturdier place on the frame, he was able to get us back out on the main road.

We turned down their invitation to stay with them for the night. I wanted to get home where Danny had clean diapers. He had already soaked his second set of clothes and needed a complete change.

By eleven o'clock we had gotten about half way down the next cross road--only 1¼ miles from home. A car sat across the road ahead of us; another one was visible just beyond it, also crosswise of the road. We could go no farther. We had already passed five ditched cars in the last half mile. As we stopped, the car slid sideways on the domed road and came to rest rear-end in the ditch.

We had no choice but to abandon the car and walk the rest of the way home. Frank wrapped Danny in a small blanket I kept in the car for him to sleep on and carried him--fighting and screaming--as I followed behind.

By then the snow was waist deep to me. We struggled through the drifts as the wind penetrated to our bones. I had never been so cold. No coat, no boots--just a light cotton skirt and blouse. After all, it had been 70 degrees when we left home.

My feet were numb by the time we reached my house. The warm air made my face and hands feel as if they were on fire. Luckily, neither of us had any frost bite. After I bathed Danny in warm water, changed his clothes, fed him, and put him down to sleep, I fixed some hot soup for Frank and me to help warm us up.

I don't know what the neighbors thought that night--and I didn't care. Frank was going to walk the other 1½ miles to where he was staying and I insisted that he stay and sleep on the couch. He had had enough cold for one night. And besides, he had to help me go and get my car the next day.

MY MICHIGAN

Have you ever been to Michigan
When spring was in the air
And every time you turned around
You found a new leaf there?

Have you ever been in Michigan
In summer's golden light
And seen the beauty of the flowers--
The beauty of the night?

Have you ever been in Michigan
When fall was shining through
With harvests of our fruits and corn
And trees of every hue?

Have you ever been in Michigan
On some still winter night
And seen the beauty of the land
All blanketed in white?

God's always been in Michigan.
He's made its beauty shine.
That's why I love the old sweet state
And why I call it mine.

MY NOTES AND THOUGHTS

THROUGH THE YEAR

THE BOOK: Start the year by considering the promise and exciting possibilities of the 365 days ahead, forgetting about the past, and joyfully using each day you are given.

MEMORY OF THE SENSES: A sensual tour through all four seasons.

VALENTINE SURPRISE: A fun look at Valentine's Day.

EASTER HAS A MEANING: Easter is not all about bunnies and colored eggs. Here is the real reason for the celebration: Christ died on the cross for us--and then He rose from the dead!

E-A-S-T-E-R: An acrostic poem, following the pattern of many of the psalms, in which the first letter of each verse is a letter in a word: in this case, "Easter".

SPRINGTIME ON THE MOUNTAIN: A look at Spring as it arrives on the Cumberland Plateau in Tennessee.

PEACE: These are the things which bring peace to my heart.

FATHERS: A tribute to all fathers on their special day.

OCTOBER 31: An alliterative word play on the eve of All Saint's Day.

OPRYLAND COUNTRY CHRISTMAS: The Opryland Hotel in Nashville, Tennessee, is changed into a wonderland of twinkling lights at Christmas time. I wrote this poem when Opryland Park was still open and contained beautiful Christmas displays, also.

CHRISTIAN DREAMER: Another poem written when I was 15. Let us not forget the real meaning of Christmas and the One whose birthday we celebrate.

THE BOOK

At the beginning of each year we are handed a blank book--365 pages to write in as we please. Each day is a new page--clean, untouched, waiting to be filled with joy or sadness, thoughtfulness or abandon, friends or enemies, comfort or pain.

Last year's book is finished. We are not allowed to go back and rewrite the manuscript, although we can sometimes add a footnote to a page which seems incomplete.

We can re-read some sections to refresh our memories and give us inspiration for today's writing. But we must not dwell there or this year's book will be but just a copy. There is no progress in repeating old mistakes, and old pleasures seem stale if they become routine.

Each of us has his own book. Each will write his own version of the days that pass. No two books will be the same.

We have control over how the pages are filled. Although a page may be stained by a teardrop or a smear of blood--or even be ripped apart--by influences over which we have no control, we are the ones who put the words on the page. We decide how these events affect our story. Do we allow them to direct our thinking, and therefore our script? Or do we wipe off the tear, write around the blood stain, tape up the torn page, and continue controlling how our story is written?

We can write by the bright sunlight of hope and inner peace, or bury ourselves in a dungeon of melancholy and despair. Even though some pages are written in the dark, each new day brings a new and blank page. We can begin again in better light if we so choose.

Some pages will be filled with new friends, new skills mastered, dreams come true; some with family lost, broken promises, and illness. But when the book is finished after 365 days, if the good pages out-number the bad, we can truly say, "It's been a very good year."

MEMORY OF THE SENSES

Many of my childhood memories are inescapably connected with the sights, sounds, and smells of the seasons of the year. Each has its distinctive characteristics.

SPRING: Violets and daffodils cascading down a hillside; the faint scent of lilacs wafting on a breeze; rain drops tap-dancing on a tin roof; the feel of newly-plowed earth on bare feet; beating the rugs to dislodge a winter's accumulation of dirt.

SUMMER: lace curtains filtering the afternoon sun; the fresh clean smell of line-dried sheets mixed with the aroma of new-mown hay; a whip-poor-will's solo above a bull-frog choir; the feel of cool well water on a sun-parched brow; the taste of a cool watermelon.

FALL: hillsides aflame with nature's palette; the pungent odor of burning leaves; the taste of fresh-squeezed cider; the steady rhythm of the woodsman's axe as he stocks a winter's supply of fuel; crisp, cool evening air--just right for a denim jacket.

WINTER: shirts freeze-drying on the line; the smell of wood burning in a pot-bellied stove; the sparkling crunch of new-fallen snow; the warmth of flannel sheets on a feather bed.

Your senses may have different connections with the past, but when you see, smell, hear, or feel something which brings back a flood of memories, you are not alone.

VALENTINE SURPRISE

My honey sent a valentine--
I was so thrilled that he was mine--
I opened it--a great surprise!
For there in hearts before my eyes,
With hugs and kisses all aflame,
He wrote in someone else's name!!!

EASTER HAS A MEANING

Easter has a meaning.
What does it mean to you?
Does it mean Easter bunnies
And eggs and candy, too?
Does it mean a day of play
And laughs and drinks and fun?
Or does it mean a day to pray
And thank God for His Son?

Easter has a meaning--
The difference in the eye
Of one who does the wondering
Of where those meanings lie.
One will say, "A day of glee
Is what our Easter means."
Some people think it fun to see
Who first can burst his seams.

Easter has a meaning--
A meaning good and true;
When Jesus died for sinners,
He died for me and you.
When we think of Easter day,
We think of God's great Son
Who died to wash our sins away,
And loved us every one.

EASTER

Each and every one of us
In God's world here below,
Had really ought to know
Christ the Lord was crucified
Because He loved us so.

At the cross on Calvary
Our Jesus bled and died.
The soldiers stabbed His side.
He forgave them even then
And later knew they cried.

Silently their way they made
To where our Jesus lay.
They honored Him that day
'Cause He arose to show the world
He loved us as they say.

To the cross on Calvary
I always will be true.
I think that you should, too.
Many times I've seen His love
Work wonders--not a few.

Easter is day for praise--
To come and praise His name.
He rose to unknown fame
When He gave His precious life
To save us from Hell's flame.

Raise you voice in prayer to Him
At morning, noon, and night.
You know that He is right.
You will always find Him there
In God's fair Heavenly light.

SPRINGTIME ON THE MOUNTAIN

When it's springtime on the mountain
And Winter says goodbye,
God waves His hand and warms the land
Beneath the sunny sky.

The frothy pink of redbuds,
And bluebirds on the wing;
I stroll across the furry moss,
And hear the robins sing.

A snowy splash of dogwood
Is sprinkled through the pines,
And my heart thrills to daffodils
That march in yellow lines.

The water flows in rivulets
As icy springs unfreeze,
And purple sets of violets
Beneath the greening trees.

It's springtime on the mountain,
And breezes bring the news,
As Nature smiles across the miles
To chase the winter blues.

PEACE

Peace to me will always be
A moon-lit summer night,
With piercing trill of Whip-poor-will,
And fire-flies in flight.

Or drizzling rain on window pane;
A baby fast asleep;
A morning jog with friendly dog;
Fish swimming in the deep.

A babbling brook with flower'd nook
In springtime woods; I meet
A spotted fawn--bird songs at dawn;
Soft moss beneath my feet.

I try to cling to peaceful things
When troubles 'round me reign.
As down life's road travails explode
To cause me grief and pain.

Above the din my Lord came in:
He dwells within my heart.
'Tho wars surround, my soul has found
His peace will not depart.

IT'S FATHER

Who makes the money
On which we live?
And that we take
More than we give?
It's Father

Who played with us
When we were young,
And taught us how
To use our tongue?
It's Father.

Who paints the house
And makes repairs
On sticking knobs
And kitchen chairs
It's father.

Who said to go to
Bed at night,
And told us what
Was wrong and right?
It's Father.

Sometimes he'll
Threaten and complain
But quick's a wink
He's calm again.
That's Father.

OCTOBER 31

Ghostly greenish goblins

Gambol in the grass.

Plump imported pumpkins

Piled too high to pass.

Wicked wailing witches

Wait in wiggly hats.

Kids in crazy costumes

Carry hairy cats.

Bloody barking banshees

Bellow as they brood.

Magic midnight moonlight

Magnifies the mood.

Lazy, lethal lions

Languishing and lean.

Haunted harvest haystacks:

HOORAY! IT'S HALLOWEEN!

OPRYLAND COUNTRY CHRISTMAS

Millions of miniature star-lights
Turn the trees into crystal and gold,
Creating a fairytale funland--
A wondrous sight to behold.

A mountain of scarlet poinsettias,
And waters that dance in the night,
Keeping time to the music of harp strings,
Set afire by a beamed laser light.

A riverboat ride in the sunshine,
A manger and angels like milk,
A beautiful tropical garden,
And fish with the colors of silk.

Surrounded by sights of the season;

Transported by music and dance;

Cuisine that has raptured the taste buds,

Hot cider and reindeer that prance.

But every dream has an ending;

I slowly retrace where I've been;

Pack memories of magic and glitter,

And return to the real world again.

CHRISTIAN DREAMER

As I sit here at the window
Looking out across the snow,
I can hear the pine-tree singing,
Fingered by the wind's brisk blow,
As I listen to the music--
Sweet and soft--it fills the ears--
I remember how the angels sang
When shepherds showed their fears.

As I sit here at the window
Watching snow come tumbling down,
I can also see dear Mary
As she rode into the town;
Joseph also is there with her
As they go from place to place,
Hunting for a little shelter
'Till His birth they have to face.

As I sit here at the window

Thinking of God's gift of love,

I can see the Wise Men coming:

See the star way up above?

How they loved Him! How they hunted

For the place where Jesus lay

So that they could give Him frankincense

And gold and myrrh that day.

Of all these I am reminded

As I look across the snow

'Cause I know Christmas is coming

And we mortals here below

Will once again come praise Him

For His tender, loving care

And spread His blessed tidings

Here and there and everywhere.

MY NOTES AND THOUGHTS

ALL NATURE SINGS

I wrote the nature poems included in this section to accompany a slide show presentation. Share them with a friend. Close your eyes and paint a picture in your mind to match the word pictures as they are read.

THE ICE STORM: On New Year's Eve, 1980, we had a sleet storm which resulted in 1 ½ inches of ice on every tree and twig. When the sun came out, the scene was enchanting.

SNOW: What would a northern winter be without snow? Some years the snow which fell in November was still on the ground in April--with lots more on top.

WIND: March is known for wind. You can't see it, but you can sure see what it does and where it has been, as in the case of a tornado.

SPRING FLOWERS: The awakening of the blooming trees is a promise of more abundance to come.

WATERFALLS: I am fascinated by waterfalls, from tiny rivulets to giant torrents like Niagara Falls.

CLOUDS: We used to lay on our back and try to determine the pictures in the cloud formations. But clouds can have a dark side, too, and tell a story of their own.

FALL LEAVES: One of the most colorful times of the year. Fall can be fun for kids jumping in leaf piles and frustrating for dads raking up those leaves.

SUNSETS: Some days close out in a blaze of glory. The old adage holds true: "Red at night, sailor's delight".

REFLECTIONS: Close your eyes and picture a shoreline with a forest ablaze in fall foliage marching down to the water's edge, blue sky up above: and all of it reflected in perfect detail in the lake's quiet waters.

HOW CAN ONE DENY? With all that God has given us to show the beauty of His creation, how can anyone deny that He exists?

THE ICE STORM

Shimmering crystalline wonderland,
Delicate magical lace,
Miniature silvery waterfalls,
Frozen in time and space.

Dazzling filigree statuettes,
Mystical glassmaker's fun,
Beautiful colorless overcoats
Glittering in the sun.

SNOW

Meadows blanketed in goose-down;
Brilliant white-on-white.
Fluffy comforter of sea-foam
Frozen in its flight.
Sparrows struggle,
Squirrels snuggle;
Tucked in for the night.

Snowflakes dancing on the window;
Symphony to please.
Drifts are shifting, slowly sifting,
Driven on the breeze.
Children shiver,
Snow birds quiver;
Bundled in the trees.

WIND

Oh, wind, you're such a fickle thing;
Holding high the kites of spring
With just a brisk and lively breeze--
Then tossing cars, uprooting trees.
You fill the softly billowed sail--
Then blow the sea into a gale.
The flowers nod as you pass by;
You cause the stately pines to sigh.
And then, without a word, you change--
Become tornados, hurricanes.
With howling voice you drive the snow;
Yet, no one sees you as you go.
You gently lift the feathered wing.
Yes, wind, you are a fickle thing.

SPRING FLOWERS

The world awakes and bursts to glory,
Promises of life to come.
O'er winter's death the spring flowers blooming
Celebrate the victory won.

Meadows washed with vibrant rainbows;
Multitude of colors rare.
Beneath the lovely glowing petals--
Summer's harvest hidden there.

WATERFALLS

Tumbling torrents,
Roaring down the mountain sides,
Splashing where the sturgeon hides,
Washing rugged cliffs and rocks,
Grand cascades that nothing blocks,
Currents where the flotsam rides.

Racing rivulets,
Streaming midst the rooted trees,
Bouncing' round their knarled knees,
Carving thru a wooded vale,
Flowing near the shadowed trail,
Running down to silvery seas.

CLOUDS

Clouds form a canopy of cotton;
Wistful images,
Changing at the whimsy of the wind.

Soon they are threatening and brooding;
Boiling thunderheads,
Warning of the destiny to come.

Silver-lined pillows for the angels;
Strange and mystical;
Brush strokes on the canvas of the sky.

REFLECTIONS

Mirror images of beauty;
Double pleasure--double view.
Heightened sky and deepened water;
Duplicates in shades of blue.

Corners where God made His playground;
Upside down and inside out.
See the hall of magic mirrors
Play a game of turn-about.

FALL LEAVES

Hillsides flaming in the sunlight;
Shiny scarlet, glowing gold.
Stately trees adorned for Autumn,
Stand arrayed in colors bold.

Oaks awash in rust and amber,
Maples in their russet gowns.
See how length'ning days can make them
Slowly fade to burnished brown.

SUNSETS

Glowing scarlet rivers
Flow like lava thru the sky;
Skinny purple fingers
Reach to hold the day gone by.

Streams of gold and amber,
Rays of lavender and pink;
Shining sun-dip'd brushes
Paint the sky with velvet ink.

Promises of evening,
As the fiery sun is set;
Dawn brings new tomorrows,
Full of hope and no regret.

HOW CAN ONE DENY?

How can one deny,
Looking at the clouded shy,
Or in the early spring,
List'ning as the robin sings,
See the farmer in his field
Planting for the harvest yield--
How can one deny that there is God?

How can one deny,
Watching eagles soaring high--
See the flaming leaves of fall-
Rainbow arching over all--
Vistas change as seasons pass--
Flowers blooming in the grass--
How can one deny that there is God?

MY NOTES AND THOUGHTS

My Notes and Thoughts

A DIFFERENT WAY TO LOOK AT LIFE

Sometimes a word or phrase will catch my attention and stick in the back of my brain, stewing and marinating until it finally flashes into my consciousness (usually in the middle of the night) as a full-blown poem which demands that I immediately write it down before it slips back into obscurity.

UPS AND DOWNS: We've all been there--things are going well and then an unpredictable snag comes which knocks the wind out of us. Or we are feeling down and out until we hear some good news or an encouraging word which puts us back on top.

THISTLES AND THORNS: A poetic look at trials and tribulations down through the ages.

DETOURS: So many times I have made plans with the best of intentions only to have everything to wrong. Then I have had to go in a different direction which turned out to be much better in the long run--God's plan!

SHIPS AND CHRISTIANS: The first two lines of this poem come from a sermon. It got me thinking about how Christians would compare to a ship.

THE BIBLE ON STEROIDS: Some of us "old fogies" have a hard time adjusting to the concept of "Contemporary Worship" as it is done in some churches.

I CAN'T LOSE: An up-beat look at life as a Christian. "If God is for us, who can be against us?"

NEXT: The world seems to be full of situations where we have to "hurry up and wait". But there will come a time when all waiting is over.

I ASKED, I FOLLOWED: A series of bad decisions, which taught me some hard-learned lessons, reminded me where to go for the wisest advice.

SECOND FIDDLE: Not everyone can be the leader. Some of us have to follow. Every instrument in an orchestra is important, just as each organ in the body plays a vital role.

UPS AND DOWNS

Those who have lived in the lowest depths
Will rise to the highest heights.
Those who are shining with light from within
Have come thru the darkest nights.

Those who have suffered the pain of loss
Will someday be filled with joy.
Broken and hurting, they come to God:
He gives them His only Boy.

Those who have wallowed in mud and slime
Are washed to be white as snow.
Knowing that Jesus endured the cross
Can set a new life aglow.

Jesus can heal every broken life;
We know that He understands:
All of the agony, fear, and strife
Are healed by the touch of His hands.

THISTLES AND THORNS

Briers and brambles,
Thistles and thorns,
Are part of our world
From the day we are born.

The garden of Eden
Had no thorns or briers
'Til Adam and Eve bit
And proved they were liars.

Israel crossed Jordan,
Canaan to claim
But ran into troubles
With brambles to blame.

Paul the apostle
With a thorn in his side
Asked God to remove it,
And God said, "Abide."

God's only Son, Jesus,
Wore thorns as a crown;
But Satan's best efforts
Could not hold Him down.

The bramble of passion,
The briar of pride,
The seeds of destruction
Are spread far and wide.

The thistle of smugness,
The thorn of despair,
Bring them to Jesus
And then leave them there.

We, as God's children,
Are constantly warned:
Beware of the tangle
Of thistles and thorns.

DETOURS

"I know exactly what I want
And what I'm going to do.
I've planned it out, there is no doubt.
I've really thought it through."

And God in heaven gazed below.
Then smiled and shook His head.
"You've no idea what's to come."
In love, He gently said.

A loss of job, rebellious child,
And conflict in the church,
Financial woes, death of a spouse,
All left me in the lurch.

So as I've walked the road of life
My plans have had to change.
The ruts of sorrow, bumps of grief
My path did rearrange.

But through the detours I have made
I've learned to trust His scheme.
I know His path's a better one
Than I could ever dream.

SHIPS AND CHRISTIANS

A ship is not made to sit safe in the harbor;
It's made to be out on the stormy seas,
Aiming for port thru the waves with its cargo,
Muscling on 'spite the gales and the lees.

If it sits in the dock for too long it will fester,
Its hull turning slowly to buckets of rust.
It needs to be out on the waves doing battle,
Keeping the promise and earning the trust.

A Christian's not meant to rest solely in church pew,
Enjoying the sermon and singing the hymns;
He needs to be out in the field for the harvest,
Sharing the gospel and bringing them in.

The worship important, the fellowship warming,
But just as essential the living each day.
Go out in the world and face all your trials,
Show Jesus to others you meet on the way.

THE BIBLE ON STEROIDS

These are the days of "supersized",
"Improved", "exciting", "new"--
Of six-pack abs and pecks of steel,
And clothes held on with glue.

Our bodies thin, our hair puffed out--
We'd never buck the trend
Of faster cars and fancy bars--
Where will "improvements" end?

Sometimes I think our churches, too,
Are following the crowd.
What e'er it takes to bring 'em in--
Let's play that music LOUD!

Let's change a little here and there
To make the words appeal.
We wouldn't want to step on toes--
We care how people feel.

But Jesus said, "Don't change the Word,
God's message stays the same.
Don't add, subtract, or pump it up,
Or pick and rearrange."

The Bible doesn't need to change.
It stands throughout the years.
The plain and simple Word of God
Won't fall on deafened ears.

I CAN'T LOSE

I am so thankful for your loving prayers--
Your kind concern is comforting to me--
But dry your eyes and smile in Jesus' love,
Don't worry 'bout a future we can't see.

No matter how the Lord decides my fate,
I just can't lose, no matter how it ends;
For I will praise Him for His healing grace
If in His will He makes me whole again.

But if His path for me is Heaven's gate,
Then in His arms I'll rest forever more
And praise Him then for bringing me back home--
For now or later, I will cross that shore.

My heart is peaceful and my mind's at ease,
For God's in charge and I will let Him choose--
My broken mind and body He will heal,
Or take me home to Heaven--I can't lose!

NEXT

I'm sitting in the waiting room,
The hour is drawing near,
Then someone comes and says, "You're next",
And it's my turn, I fear.

Or standing in the movie line,
I'm getting mighty vexed.
It's moving at a turtle's pace--
I wish that I were next.

I think about the many times
I nearly came in last,
When being next was out of reach--
The chance already passed.

I've studied well the Bible's text
And eagerly await
For Jesus' gently whispered, "Next--
I'll meet you at the Gate."

I'll enter into Heaven's fold
To glory so sublime.
I'll praise His name and shout, "Hurrah!"
No longer next in line.

I ASKED, I FOLLOWED

I asked my heart what I should do,
My heart said, "Love's the thing
That stars the eye, makes breezes sigh,
And causes birds to sing.
So follow love where e'er it leads,
Enjoy the moments rare.
Pursue the joy of girl and boy,
And live without a care."

I followed my heart and it let me down.
It caused me sorrow and pain.
For desires of the heart
Are not very smart;
And rose-colored dreams are in vain.

I asked my head what I should do;
My head said, "Think, don't feel.
Just search your mind, and you will find
An answer that is real.
Forget the dreams of foolish men;
Look only for the truth;
You'll never fall if you'll recall
The lessons of your youth."

I followed my head and it let me down.

My life was useless and cold.

For the thoughts of the head

Left me lonely instead

Of turning my wishes to gold.

I asked my God what I should do,

And He said, "Kneel and pray.

Then hear my voice, I'll guide your choice,

And lead you through the day."

He gave me hope. He gave me peace.

He gave me eyes that see.

And now I know, where e'er I go,

I'll find what's best for me.

I followed my God, tho' the path was rough;

At times I stumbled and fell.

But the touch of His hand

Pulled me up, helped me stand;

And now in contentment I dwell.

SECOND FIDDLE

Someone once asked Leonard Bernstein what was the most difficult position in the orchestra for someone to hold. He replied, "That's easy--it's second fiddle. No one wants to play second fiddle." What a comment on humanity in general!

No one wants to play second fiddle. We all have that need to feel important. Some of us have a much stronger desire than others to be the "big shot", but everyone--at some time or another--has an ego problem.

There is a popular bumper sticker that states, "God is my co-pilot". Many good Christians feel that this is a statement to the world of their faith. But, think about it: how preposterous! If God is the co-pilot, then we're the pilot. That's backwards! God has to be the pilot of our lives. We need to follow His lead, not the other way around.

As in the orchestra, the first fiddle takes the lead, and the second fiddle fills in the harmony--so in life God is the leader and we create the harmony with our words and deeds. As long as each instrument in the orchestra plays its proper part, under the leadership of the conductor, the music is harmonious and gentle on the ears.

How beautiful and harmonious this world could be if everyone played his/her part, under God's leadership. We each have a specific part to play in God's plan--and for most of us, it will be "second fiddle"--but not second in importance. Just as each instrument in the orchestra is necessary for the sound of the whole, so each of us is an integral and important part of God's plan.

Let's pray that we can find our part and play it for His glory!

MY NOTES AND THOUGHTS

BECAUSE I HAVE LOVED

THE WALL: I believe that many people have built a protective wall after being disappointed and hurt by someone whom they loved and trusted. It can become very lonely inside that wall.

LONELINESS: Who hasn't felt lonely at some time? Often we make poor decisions because of loneliness.

TO MY FRIEND: A true friend is a rare find. Some of my friends have been closer than any family member.

COMMUNICATION: I have learned that a friendship or a loving relationship cannot survive for long without honest communication.

I DON'T KNOW YOU: I wrote this poem when my current husband and I were getting acquainted by phone. We met through an ad in a Christian singles magazine.

LOVE IS A VERB: Love is an over-used word in the English language. The only kind of love that has any meaning is love in action.

NIGHT SOUNDS: A loving couple stroll beside still waters and share a symphony of evening sights and sounds.

HORIZONS: Sharing quiet times with a loved one and looking forward to the future together.

LOVER'S PRAYER: Every relationship should have God at the center. This prayer has been used at a few weddings.

HOW COULD YOU? When my late husband, Dick, died suddenly and unexpectedly of a heart attack, I went through a very depressing time. Writing my feelings down helped me get past the anger stage of grief.

'TIL THEY'RE GONE: A friend of mine, Thelma Ford, whose husband had died, shared with me how hard it had been for her to cope with his snoring--until he was gone and she discovered that it was the thing which she missed the most.

THE WALL

I built a wall around myself,
So high and strong and wide--
To shut the hurt away from me
And keep me safe inside.

I built a wall around myself
And let nobody in.
I closed my heart and told my mind
That happiness was sin.

I built a wall around myself,
But learned to my dismay;
The fort that shut the others out
Just kept me penned away.

That wall I built around myself
Became a prison cold.
No longer free to think or feel,
I opened up the fold.

Without the wall around myself,
My heart was free to soar,
And when I let my Lord come in
Love knocked upon my door.

LONELINESS

Loneliness is empty hours
With no one near to share
The passing of eternal time--
Lost castles in the air.

Loneliness is shattered dreams
Left blowing in the wind,
The loss of one who was the rock
To which your hopes were pinned.

Loneliness can drain the heart
And leave it worn and scarred--
An empty vase--a fragile shell--
Or icy cold and hard.

Loneliness does have one cure--
It's not a fatal end.
It's gone that joyous, sunny day
You find a special friend.

TO MY FRIEND

I needed help and called on you,
And quickly you were there.
You cheered me up when I was blue
And showed me that you care.

'Tho I don't ask, you seem to know
Just when I need a smile.
When I'm alone, you call me up
And talk to me awhile.

You know my faults, you even share
Some secrets that I've told,
And yet you like me anyhow;
Your heart is solid gold.

I'm glad I met someone like you
Before my journey's end.
The world is brighter for me now,
Because you are my friend.

COMMUNICATION

We chat about the weather,
Reminisce of yesterdays,
Describe in finest detail
Our youthful escapades;
We analyze our motives,
Discuss the books we've read;
But important thoughts and feelings
Are often left unsaid.

We share the same opinions
On politics and wars,
Our conversation touches
On people, places, cars;
We strive for understanding;
Talk together on the way;
But the words that really matter
Are the ones we never say.

I can't read your thought-waves--
The things you'd like to do--
Just as mine are also hidden
And a mystery to you;
We're missing the completeness
That could brighten every day--
A loss of precious closeness
Because of things we didn't say.

I DON'T KNOW YOU

I don't really know you,
Though I've talked with you awhile.
As I've listened to your message,
In your voice I've heard a smile.

I have never seen you,
But I feel our hearts have met.
And if we don't pursue it,
We may live with sad regret.

Though I've never touched you,
Never walked with arms entwined,
You are here forever near me
In the pathways of my mind.

We have the same ambitions,
Our thoughts sing a duet,
Our minds already partners--
But I don't know you--yet.

LOVE IS A VERB

Love is something you do
For someone who is dear.
What good is a car if the motor runs
But you never put it in gear?

Love's a verb--not a noun.
It's not unlike a bell
That hangs on a pole and will never be heard--
'Till it moves, no message can tell.

Love is an empty word
That falls on deafened ears;
Unless there is action to show the world
What you say is really sincere.

Love is the way you treat
The ones you meet each day.
I look at the deeds that you do--or don't--
And I really can't hear what you say.

NIGHT SOUNDS

Hand in hand we stroll along
Beside the moon-lit waters, deep,
And hear the earth burst forth in song.
Begins the evening symphony.

Crickets fiddle their refrain--
A strong staccato harmony--
From under cozy rocks and logs.
And from the lily pads, the frogs

Bellow mellow tuba notes,
While thru the trees a gentle breeze
Carries toad-sung melodies
To shadowed men in fishing boats.

The echoed trill of "Whip-poor-will"
Announcing his identity
In answer to a nosy owl
Who questions from a willow tree..

We stand together, arms entwined--
The rhythm of your beating heart
Combines with mine--becomes a part--
And I thank God for night sounds.

HORIZONS

Ahead of us
The earth recedes,
Promising new sights, new sounds,
New pleasures.
On the horizon, silver-lined clouds
Create moving pictures
Of possibilities--
Of dreams as yet unlived.

The sun sets,
And above the horizon
Myriad colors glow and change.
Intertwining rivers of mem'ries,
Reminding us of former days,
Gone, but not forgotten.
Tho' traces remain, they slowly fade.
'Till darkness descends
And paints in shades of black and grey,
Irregular shadows,
Where earth and sky combine
Becoming one.
As we walk, and talk, and dream.
Of new horizons.

A LOVER'S PRAYER

Dear Lord,

It never ceases to amaze us how we found each other in that million-piece jig-saw puzzle of lost and lonely souls out there: two minds and hearts of a kind finding each other against such great odds. Thank you, God.

Thank you for brilliant sunsets that inspire our hearts to soar in gratitude; for soft sunrises that promise us a new day--every day--to correct the mistakes of the past and build memories for the future; for the trials in our lives which make us stronger, draw us closer, and help us to appreciate the good times; for mountains and valleys; for all of Your creation that we can enjoy together; for family, and friends, and home. Most of all, thank you for Your Son Who is always with us.

We pray for eyes that see, ears that hear, and hearts that understand as we try to make sense of the state of "togetherness".

Give us the proper words to offer comfort in times of sorrow, encouragement in times of distress, hope in times of despair, and joy in times of celebration.

May we keep each other from stumbling on the rocky road of life; always there with a strong arm to lean on and a shoulder to cry on. Let us remember that You are always there to lead us through all the pitfalls, if we will only ask for Your guidance.

Remind us daily that true love is unselfish, honest, honorable, tender, constant, and--most of all--patient.

Help us to find, accept, and follow Your will in the coming days, weeks, months, and years; putting our desires in line with Yours.

We pray all this in the name of Your Son, Jesus Christ, who--in His life and death--showed us the greatest love of all.

Amen.

HOW COULD YOU?

How could you?
How dare you leave me like that--
With no warning, no thought of the ensuing void?
No time to prepare my mind for the details--
        The paperwork
                The never-ending paperwork.
Why didn't you think ahead?
You could have made preparations.
Then I wouldn't have been faced with those endless decisions
        at a time when my mind and soul were numb.
Or did their necessity force me to function
When I would rather have withdrawn from the world?
        Crawled into a shell--
                A coffin of my own making.
Why did you wait?
Did you think you would live forever?
You could have saved some money
Instead of buying all those things--
        Those lovely things--
                All gone now to pay the bills--
                        An endless procession of bills.
How could you?
We were two unhappy souls
        Dejected and rejected
When we finally found each other.
We had such a short time together--
        (Was it really all of 13 years?)
Why did you have to leave so soon?
What right did you have to take away:
        The moonlit walks hand-in-hand,
        The joy of dancing to a country band,
        The quiet talks by a glowing fire,
        The honeyed soothing of our desire?

You took it all away--
And left nothing but a bottomless pit.
Nothing to hang onto--
 Except memories--
  Sweet, sweet memories.
I don't want memories.
 They hurt too much.
I want anger--
 Vile, vicious anger.
I want to rant and rave and throw things--
Watch them shatter like the pieces of my life--
 Cold, meaningless shards.
You had no right to leave me alone to face the world.
Yes, I faced it alone before--
 Before you.
Before I learned what a comfort it could be
 To share the burden,
 To have a shoulder to cry on,
 To have someone who cared.
But you spoiled me.
You taught me to depend on you--
 Your love,
 Your patience,
 Your strength and kindness.
Then you snatched it away in one fleeting second--
 Left me here floundering and alone.
How could you?
If only the anger would come and stay--
 Then maybe--
  Just maybe--
This heart-rending pain would go away.

'TIL THEY'RE GONE

Diaper pails and sterile bottles,
Cotton tube socks wrapped in pairs,
Muddy foot prints in the hallway,
Chocolate thumb marks on the chairs,
Mornings filled with tears and squabbles,
Tinker toys out on the lawn;
How I fussed and tried to change things;
And yet I miss them--now they're gone.

Sawdust sifting from shirt pockets,
Cigarettes and frothy beers,
Nightly snoring that I hated,
Now'd be music to my ears.
Toothpaste tubes all bent and mangled,
Fishing trips at break of dawn,
Piles of tools upon my table,
Oh, how I miss them--since they're gone.

All the minor irritations
That we live with every day
Sometimes seem to overwhelm us,
And we wish they'd go away.
But be careful what you wish for,
Lest you find some breaking dawn
No one left to cause you problems--
You'll never miss them--'till they're gone.

MY NOTES AND THOUGHTS

MY NOTES AND THOUGHTS

THERE'S MORE TO THE STORY

THE WHITTLER: At a local craft show, I was observing many people watching a friend of mine, Casto Greene, who was one of the co-founders of the local Crossville Carving Club, whittle wonderful figures out of pieces of wood. I wrote this especially for him.

THE BURDEN OF THE CROSS: A friend was telling me about a lady who was having a difficult time dealing with the burden of the "cross" she had to bear. The phrase started the "creative juices" flowing.

INNOCENCE IS GONE: Written immediately after 9-11-2001, these thoughts came rolling out rather quickly. Those horrible images will be forever etched in memories all over the world.

THE HEDGE: God puts a hedge of protection around His people. Are we still His people, or have we strayed too far away? Something to ponder.

BIRD FEATHERS: When my granddaughter, Jade, graduated from high school, I gave her a brooch made out of a lovely feather. This poem went with the pin.

RUST AND SOOT AND SQUIRREL'S NESTS: I wrote this poem to use along with a Bible study for a Women's Retreat for our church.

ON THINGS THAT LAST: Vern and Betty Thalmann, some friends of mine, were celebrating their 25th anniversary. Betty had always wanted an antique silver castor set. I managed to find one, and we gave it to them accompanied by this framed poem.

THOSE WHO'VE GONE BEFORE: I initially wrote this for a lady in our church whose sister had died. Since then I have included it when I have sent sympathy cards to those who have lost loved ones.

THE WHITTLER

I pick a block from off the pile
And search to see its soul.
Inside the wood a mystery hides--
To find it is my goal.

I take my knife and start to carve
A little here and there.
As shavings fall around my feet,
I whittle now with care.

Don't take too much, but just enough--
Be careful not to slip.
I wouldn't want to leave a mark--
Or lose a finger tip.

And there it is--the final form,
The task at last is done.
The figure hidden deep within
Came out to see the sun.

THE BURDEN OF THE CROSS

The crowd was milling aimlessly;
The people pushed and shoved
To see the man who claimed to be
The promise of God's love.

This man with dirty, tattered robe:
How could he be the One?
His face all bloody, shoulders stooped--
He's not Jehovah's Son!

He stumbled once, He stumbled twice
Beneath the heavy load.
They couldn't see the world of sin
That on His shoulders rode.

A soldier ordered, "Help him out!"
And from the gathered dross
A man stepped out and humbly shared
The burden of the cross.

* * * * *

A frightened girl in sorrow mired
Because of painful loss
Thought suicide, 'til someone shared
The burden of her cross.

Dear God, I pray, make me aware
Of those whose hope is lost;
And help me be the one to share
The burden of the cross.

INNOCENCE IS GONE

The world exploded on that day,
A million dreams were swept away,
While dread and terror held their sway
And innocence was gone.

The images of fear and pain,
The piles of rubble that remain,
And smoke unhindered by the rain
Still glowing in the dawn.

We ask, "How could it happen here?'
And, "Don't you think it's really queer
That God, Who says He's always near
Would let these acts go on?"

But He was there among the men
Who toiled for hours and failed, and then
Returned to struggle once again
'tho hope was surely gone.

Our Lord hates evil in His day,
But doesn't force us to obey,
So evil men will have their way.
For innocence is gone.

His people join to praise His name.
There is no point in spreading blame,
For all of us can share the shame
That innocence is gone.

THE HEDGE

"I will protect you, said the Lord,
"My hedge grows thick and tall.
Just do your part and praise My Name:
Obey the Shepherd's call."

"My hedge will keep the devil out.
Although he huffs and puffs,
He cannot harm your soul, your faith.
My hedge will be enough."

God's hedge protected Job and Lot,
Joseph and Israel.
But when His people turned away
The hedge protection fell.

And what about the U.S.A. ?
Our founders loved the Lord--
A nation formed to worship free
That now ignores His word.

9-11 should have been
A warning to us all
That if our country doesn't change
We know the hedge could fall.

Will He withdraw His holy hedge
Because we won't obey?
Let's lead our nation back to God.
Get on our knees and pray.

BIRD FEATHERS

The baby bird tries out her wings
And slowly learns to fly.
She sees so many wondrous things
While soaring thru the sky.

And you, just like that little bird,
One day will leave the nest,
And what you do by deed and word
Will put you to the test.

The world's a big and scary place,
And like that tiny bird,
You'll need some strength the trials to face--
Use wisdom that you've heard.

So wear this feather, girl, with pride--
It signifies my love.
Remember, God is by your side
And watching from above.

RUST AND SOOT AND SQUIRREL'S NESTS

Rust and soot and squirrel's nests
Are clogging up my flue.
And so I cannot light a fire--
Lord, show me what to do.

The rust is caused by laziness--
I know that I'm to blame--
I found excuses to ignore
When Jesus called my name.

To go and visit some lost soul
And tell of Jesus' love,
Or see and heed a neighbor's need,
Or praise the Lord above.

My sins are building up the soot
That covers deep and wide,
So people only see the dirt
And not the love inside.

I need to clean my thoughts and deeds
And keep my eyes on high
So I don't harbor angry thoughts
Or tell a little lie.

The squirrel's nests are built of things
That occupy my life
And take my time an thoughts away
And cause me endless strife.

There's home and work and meals to fix
And shopping at the store.
And I regret I soon forget
Just what God made me for.

So when I clean my chimney out
My life won't be the same
And God can send His light through me--
The world can see the flame.

ON THINGS THAT LAST

We've weathered well down through the years
Your marriage, dears, and I.
You've had your lumps, and I my bumps,
And yet we didn't die.

The shine is gone, and in its place
A luster, soft and warm,
That shows the world our lives unfurled--
We've weathered out the storm.

When I was new, your marriage, too--
We knew we were the best.
Then came the strife of daily life--
And we have stood the test.

We've seen the days that come and go--
The shifting sands of time.
Through satin sheen, a beauty seen--
We have a deeper shine.

The world can't know the things we've shared--
The places we have been--
And with the years, the joys, the tears--
We're better now that then.

THOSE WHO'VE GONE BEFORE

The rapture of spring flowers in bloom
Reminds of other times:
Of laughter, love, of family ties,
And childhood so sublime.

The gentle sound of summer rain
Reminds me of the tears
That once were shed in agony,
Now muted by the years.

Sometimes at night the mem'ries come
Of those who've gone before.
And then I long to see the ones
Who wait at Heaven's door.

I know that God my heart will heal--
He loves me even more.
One day He'll welcome me among
The ones who've gone before.

My Notes and Thoughts

MY NOTES AND THOUGHTS

OBSERVATIONS

I have learned so much about life by simply being aware of things around me. So often we look, but don't really see because we aren't paying attention.

SIMPLE THINGS: There are so many wonderful gifts that God has given us. We need to be aware of them in order to appreciate them.

MOTHERS--FATHERS--CHILDREN: A tongue-in-cheek look at the roles that each person plays in family life. The last line is so true!

YESTERDAY, TODAY, TOMORROW: There's no use worrying. Yesterday is over and done. We are not promised tomorrow. Today is all we have. Make the best of it.

PEOPLE WATCHING: I was sitting in a booth at the Cumberland County Fair watching as people passed by. It dawned on me how unique each person was, and I began to take notes.

THE STAIRWAY: I wrote this poem as a result of an assignment for the Plateau Writers. We were asked to go somewhere and observe what was going on around us. I chose to sit on a bench near a stairway in a mall.

SIMPLE THINGS

A sunny smile when you're sad and blue,
A pat on the back to cheer,
A friendly call when you're all alone,
A letter from someone dear;

A sun-tanned boy and his dog at play,
Expressing the joy within,
The gentle sound of a summer rain,
Tap dancing on roofs of tin;

A quiet walk by a moonlit lake,
The cry of a whip-poor-will,
And singing songs by a crackling fire
That chases the evening chill;

The fond caress of a lover's hand
That quiets the timid heart,
Some feathered frost on a window pane
Revealing the Master's art;

A drop of dew on a spider's web
Aglow in the golden dawn,
The majesty of a stately tree
That shelters a gentle fawn;

The simple things that make life worth-while
Are here for us all to share--
Just look and see what the Lord provides
To show that He does care!

MOTHERS--FATHERS—CHILDREN

Mothers are for smiling
And washing dirty shirts,
And sewing on a button,
And kissing where it hurts.
They clean and cook and read a book,
And catch you when you fall.
They sometimes yell, but you can tell
They love you after all.
They sing while they are driving
Or mopping up the floor.
They make you eat your carrots;
And that's what Moms are for.

Fathers are for playing
And fishing in a stream,
And building you a swing set,
And following a dream.
They sit you down, act like a clown,
And toss you overhead,
Then pat your hair and hear your prayers,
And tuck you into bed.
They take you to the circus
To hear the lions roar,
And teach you how to toss a ball,
And that's what Dads are for.

Children are for learning,
And asking, "What?" and "Why?".
Like, "Why do I have freckles?"
And, "What holds up the sky?".
They climb a tree so they can see
The mountains far away,
And in their mind they always find
A friend with whom to play.
Their favorite things are running
And slamming kitchen doors--
To drive their parents crazy--
'Cause that's what kids are for!

YESTERDAY, TODAY, TOMORROW

YESTERDAY is gone now,
'Twill never come again.
Hazy, haunting memories
Are all that still remain.
Some bring peals of laughter,
Some bring bitter tears,
Some give understanding
To swiftly fading years.

TODAY is plastic putty
We're free to shape and mold,
To paint in muted flesh tones
Or splash with colors bold.
Seconds, minutes, hours;
Each of us can fill--
With agony or pleasure--
According to our will.

TOMORROW is a dream world
That never quite arrives,
A time of misty musings
And castles in the skies.
Worry cannot change it,
Wishes, too, are vain;
Hope can bring contentment--
God's promises remain.

PEOPLE WATCHING

Some are short and some are tall,
Some look like they've hit a wall,
Some are fat and some are thin,
And one looks like he has no chin.
Hair of white and blonde and red--
Hers looks like an unmade bed--
His hair is grey and hers is brown,
She wears a smile and he a frown.
Some with glasses, some without,
Some a grin and some a pout,
Hands in pockets, gloves, or rings,
One lady struts and one just swings.
With cap or hat or balding head
Or bows and beads or locks of dred.
A happy smile from ear to ear
Or darting eyes so full of fear.
I wish I understood these things--
Why some are sad and some have wings.
With all this great variety
Surrounding us, it seems to me
That no one ever should be bored.
We need to praise and thank the Lord
For making every one of us
Our own true self--no need to fuss
About the differences we find.
For entertainment I unwind
By sitting underneath the sky
And watching people passing by.

THE STAIRWAY

A toddler tries the stairs, fascinated by the sense of adventure. Tentatively, he reaches for the first step with his ever-exploring hands. His knees follow as his hands reach ever upward. One step, two, three. He glances behind, realizes where he is, sits down, and squeals with glee. His laughter turns to tears as his mother picks him up and takes him to a safer area.

Children play on the stairs: playing tag, toting toys up and down, peeking through the railing at the changing scenes below. To them, the stairway can be a mountain, a slide, a balcony, or just a way to get from here to there.

A young man takes the steps two at a time, anxious to keep an important appointment. His energy carries him onward so swiftly that the stairway seems to disappear--only a slight impediment to his progress.

A middle-aged woman carries her packages carefully as she descends, stepping heavily beneath their weight. She seems tired, moving with deliberate caution, and fumbling in her handbag with her free hand, looking for her keys.

Two men in dark suits climb in tandem, engaged in animated conversation. Their briefcases rattle against the balusters on each side, but the jarring goes unnoticed. Some important decisions must be made before they reach their destination.

An elderly lady ascends slowly, her cane in one gnarled hand, the other tightly gripping the railing. Arthritic knees barely support her as she struggles agonizingly upward. After every few steps she pauses, catching her breath. As she reaches the top, she heaves a sigh of relief.

And so goes a day in the life of a stairway.

My Notes and Thoughts

MISSION MEMORIES

Some of the greatest joys of my life have come from the various mission trips on which I have been able to go. As a part of both a Baptist building team and a Baptist Disaster Relief team, there have been many opportunities to be of aid and comfort to people in need. I truly receive much more than I give. These are some of my memories of such joys.

JOURNAL OF A MISSION IN THE MOUNTIANS: This is a journal which I wrote as a group of us traveled to Everett, Pennsylvania, to work on a neglected church building which was badly in need of some tender, loving, care.

GRATEFUL SERVANTS: My first mission building trip to Iowa was capped off by a cook-out at someone's home on the final evening. All were asked to present something special about their week. This was my contribution.

IT'S ALL ABOUT THE PEOPLE: Memories of the wonderful people I met when I was on a Disaster Relief mission trip to Atmore, Alabama, after Hurricane Ivan devastated that little town in 2005.

SYMBOL OF HOPE: A tiny tree in the parking lot of the church in which we stayed in Atmore, Alabama, during our mission trip there became the symbol of the destruction--and the hope--of the town and its people.

JOURNAL OF MISSION IN THE MOUNTAIN

SATURDAY, JULY 22, 1995

We are a diverse group: four pastors, a high school student, a mechanic, a stock boy, a store clerk, an assistant professor at Roane State, a few "domestic engineers", an ex-marine, an electrician, two farmers, etc. Our ages range from 12 to 86. But we are a team.

We are called the "Tennessee Southern Baptist Brotherhood Mission Building Team". Early this morning we gather in Crossville from Cumberland County and the Sequatchie Valley to begin our journey.

Our mission this year is to go into an area near Altoona, PA, where, due to lack of funds, some churches have been allowed to deteriorate and are badly in need of repair work. We supply the labor. The church we're working on is supposed to supply the materials.

Our 6-vehicle caravan takes I-81 up the Shenandoah Valley toward Pennsylvania. To our right, the Shenandoah Mountains stretch out, barely visible behind the haze, like a sleeping giant.

At noon, we pull into a rest stop just outside on Christiansburg, VA, and step out into the blast-furnace heat. We quickly find tables under the trees and share our picnic lunch.

The scenery is a peaceful prelude to the work we are traveling to do. We reach our destination just as the searing sun is hiding its face behind the mountains to the west.

New Hope Baptist Church in Duncansville, PA, will be our base of operations while we are here. They have a large fellowship hall with a well-equipped kitchen and a much-needed shower room. Everyone brought air mattresses to throw on the floor for sleeping--except for those of us who brought R.V.s.

Last year we spent our whole week repairing this building. This time we will stay here and drive to other churches to do whatever needs to be done.

We are concerned because part of our group, four men who left separately in a motor home, have not yet arrived.

SUNDAY;

Church services at New Hope. Pastor Bob is his fiery self. It's nice to see that the church has grown since we were here last year. It is evident that efforts have been made to keep the building in good shape. That is gratifying to those of us who were here before.

This afternoon the motor home finally limps in. They have had major problems: two blown out tires, exhaust troubles, and electrical shorts. But they are here now, and everyone breathes more easily.

We get the final run-down on the work to be done. Team leaders are assigned, and volunteers are accepted for our daily devotionals.

MONDAY:

After a hearty breakfast and our usual morning devotion period, we drive the 35 miles to Everett in a downpour, hoping that the old saying, "Rain before 7, clear before 11" holds true.

The road takes us through beautiful mountain valleys and worn-out villages, past rolling farms with ancient stone houses and huge white cantilevered barns.

The church is a large brick structure, built in two stages. The main sanctuary, with its stained-glass windows and beautiful woodwork, was built in 1885. The two-story parsonage in the rear was added later and connected to the main building with a narrow fellowship hall. The parsonage is no longer used as such, but has been integrated into the use of the church.

Many years of neglect are evident. All exterior woodwork (windows, doors, porches, etc.) is badly in need of scraping and painting. Part of a porch roof needs to be replaced. Steps from the level of the church up to the rear parking area need rebuilding. A bathroom sink needs replacing. The list is long and the funds are few.

We learn that the congregation consists of fewer than 20 loyal seniors. The pastor, a stooped, frail, white-haired gentleman of 79, greets us with a cheery, "I thought you were Baptists. Why aren't you singing?" And he leads us in a few peppy choruses.

The rain clears as hoped and the work begins. Part of our crew leaves to go over to Shannon Springs Church to do some cement work and window replacement. They'll be there a couple of days if all goes well.

One of the nicest bonuses of our mission effort is meeting interesting people. Such as Shirley. She is a new member at New Hope, and a pianist--a concert pianist. She also tours the United States giving speeches and teaching seminars on hunting deer and turkeys. This is in addition to writing a newspaper sports column and free-lancing magazine articles.

Another lovely lady, Isabelle, lives next door to the church in Everett. She offers us tea, leaves a hose running for cold water to drink and for clean-ups, fixes a picnic table in the shade, and even asks us to come in and look at her home. We politely decline because of our less-than-clean condition at the time. The huge old house beckons, however, and we may find another chance at a later time.

We are well fed. The ladies of the church bring our noon meal. Today the fare is ham salad sandwiches and home-made pies. Tomorrow will be sloppy joes and salad, and we are promised spaghetti for Wednesday. Of course, cold drinks and various "snackies" accompany.

Our other meals are delightfully handled by Judy Hearndon, the wife of our Brotherhood Director, with the help of Sharon Sevier and Ortha Davenport. They use the kitchen at our host church to prepare morning and evening feasts for the workers. No one goes hungry on this crew!

TUESDAY:

We're hot and tired--but it's a good tired. We accomplished a lot today. The windows and doors are scraped and re-puttied, ready for a primer coat of paint, the stairs down from the parking lot are replaced. One porch is encased in vinyl siding and aluminum. One more to go. Two porch rails are installed--one hand rail yet to go.

All did not come easily. We were only going to replace one small section of the porch roof. But, as shingles were removed, we discovered that the entire deck was rotted out--not even safe to stand on. So....all new plywood and rafters. The porch railing which six of us spent all day yesterday scraping was not salvageable--too much rotted wood under the paint.

Willard, my husband, started to replace the sink in the ladies rest room. The old one came out easily enough, but there wasn't a hanger to fit the new one, which was acquired from a garage sale. The small local building supply didn't have one, so the pastor said he would bring one back tomorrow.

We got to see Isabelle's home this afternoon. What a treat!

She and a few ladies from her church are working on a memorial quilt to be donated to the new Everett Museum. On it are appliquéd representations of the most historical homes, businesses, and churches in the area--including the one on which we are working.

And then there are the dolls. She has over 2000 dolls, some of which are very old. She is sorting through them now, keeping a few for herself, donating some to the museum, and pricing the others for consignment sale. Dolls of every shape, size, color, and age sit on dressers, shelves, benches, and window sills. Hand painted bisque dolls, bridal dolls, puppets, dolls with china heads and cloth bodies, clowns, "personality" dolls--girls and boys--blondes, brunettes, and red-heads. Every one of them has a story. Leaving her home was not easy.

WEDNESDAY:

What a wonderful fellowship there is between Christians working together for a common goal! Men and women, young and old, experienced and learning--all of us trying to do our best to help out those who are in need.

Yesterday the Everett church ran out of funds for materials, but there were many jobs we had started and wanted to finish. So some of the workers chipped in with their own funds to help purchase the necessary supplies.

Today the pattern continues. With every job being more complicated than originally thought, the list of materials needed was greatly underestimated. More people chip in to help out.

Roy Davis, Director of Missions for Cumberland Plateau, and our designated "gopher", makes three extra trips to the building supply. We accuse him of finding excuses to go where there is an air conditioner.

At least, we're beginning to see the end. Tomorrow we should be able to complete all the jobs we've started. The porch roof is ready to shingle, the doors are all painted. The windows are scraped, primed, and ready for the final coat of paint. Because of deterioration, many of the sills needed to be filled with wood putty and sanded before priming.

I've worked myself out of a job. All the porch and stair railings are done. Because I had worked with a carpenter last year at New Hope building porch railings, I knew the procedure. So I trained two helpers this year. Now I grab a paint brush.

More fellowship again tonight as we attend services at New Hope. Several people give testimonies about how important their Christian family is to them. I agree.

The Shannon Springs team is finally finished. They had their share of troubles, too. The back-hoe that was supposed to be there Monday didn't show until today. The cement truck driver expected payment on delivery. It took several phone calls to straighten things out. But all's well now.

THURSDAY:

Another sweltering day--especially for the three pastors putting shingles on the roof. Someone makes a comment that they are on a higher level--closer to heaven than any of the rest of us. Their reply: "It feels like we're closer to someplace else!"

We finish our work and encounter a combination of delight and sadness from our new friends in Everett. Everyone is extremely pleased with what has been accomplished. But they hate to see us leave, and beg us to come back next year.

Kathy, a new member at the church, has already roasted some home-grown beef and planned on slicing it for sandwiches for tomorrow's lunch. Isabelle had planned on feeding us ice cream and cake on our last day. So there are disappointments on both sides that we finished a day early.

There are things we wish we could have done. An obvious need is the repainting of the church steeple, a lovely open bell tower that sits about 60 feet up on a very steep peak. We just don't have any safe way of reaching it. Another need is the stripping and painting of the huge hand-carved oak front doors. They have at least ten coats of paint already in place. A job for a professional--or someone with a lot of time.

One thing we can do. One of the men climbs up in the inside of the steeple and re-attaches the bell rope. At lunch time, Kathy's son rings the bell to call us in. Isabelle comments that she is delighted to hear the old bell ringing again. It had been silent for over 20 years.

Perhaps bringing life to the old bell is a sign that life can be brought back to the old church, also. We hope so. If the love that has been shown to us by these church members is carried out into the community, that bell will be calling people in from every direction by this time next year.

Parting is such sweet sorrow. Late this afternoon we say our goodbyes to the people in Everett. Tomorrow we go our separate ways.

We'll all end up back in Tennessee by Saturday night, but by different routes and at different speeds. Some are leaving by 6 a.m. and driving straight through. The two camper trailers are going to do some sight-seeing here in the morning, then go as far as Natural Bridge, VA, to spend the night, finishing the trip on Saturday.

Since our mission team members come from a wide-spread area, we don't normally see this special group of friends except on the mission trips. So we discuss having a reunion picnic at Fall Creek Falls sometime in September. By then plans will already be well on the way for our trip next year. The affirmative vote is unanimous.

Each person who came with us is eagerly looking forward to next year. And, of course, the door is always open for new people to join us. The pay is zero, but the rewards are immeasurable.

GRATEFUL SERVANTS

Anyone can praise the Lord--
Everyone should serve Him.
It doesn't matter when or how--
With warbled voice or sweated brow--
What joy it is to please Him!

Tennessee is now our home
While here on earth we wander.
We came to serve in Iowa--
A week to build and work and pray--
As heaven's gifts we ponder.

'Tho here on earth are pain and toil,
In heaven is no sadness.
From every walk of life we come;
Apartment, farm, and mobile home,
To serve our Lord with gladness.

Teacher, preacher, fireman, clown,
Student, nurse, mortician,
And banjo picker, engineer,
A plane mechanic with no fear,
Retired marine, beautician.

'Tho all of us have traveled far
We have one goal in mind:
To do our work and please the Lord,
To praise His name with one accord,
A few new friends to find.

Friends we have become, you know;
And now we are departing.
We've gotten more than we can give,
As we return to where we live,
You're pulling on our heart-strings.

IT'S ALL ABOUT THE PEOPLE

One of the reasons I enjoy being a part of both the Tennessee Baptist Builders and the Tennessee Baptist Disaster Relief Team is the good feeling I get from touching people's lives in a positive manner.

At least as rewarding to me personally is meeting some wonderfully inspirational new friends along the way.

The week I spent in Atmore, Alabama, following hurricane Ivan, was no exception. Atmore is a small Mayberry-like town in rural Escambia County, about 50 miles north of Pensacola, Florida. Virtually no building in the entire county was left untouched.

But the spirit of the people who live there, as well as those who came to help, was not to be blown away. I'd like to introduce you to a few of these special people.

Miss Rosie (age 79) and her mother, Miss Annie (age 98) live in a small frame house on a gravel side road about 5 miles from town. Miss Annie lays on the couch in the neat and clean living room, looking every inch as if she has already "passed on". Only the sparkle in her eyes and the trace of a smile on her thin lips announce that she's not quite ready to go yet. Her daughter has to do everything for her, even moving her arms and legs as necessary for comfort. There is much love in this house--love for each other and love for God.

They have lost all the food they had in the refrigerator because the electricity was off for over a week. Miss Rosie no longer drives and has to depend on the kindness of others to get groceries. The chain-saw teams have preceded us and cleared the trees from the driveway and the back door so that the home is accessible. They passed on the word that these wonderful widow ladies, who have no insurance, could use some extra help.

We bring them some boxes of M.R.E.'s (Meals Ready to Eat) to help with their dietary needs. Miss Rosie throws her hands in the air and dances around the room. "Praise God! Thank the Lord!", she cries, her lovely chocolate face radiant as she gives each of us a giant hug.

Miss Annie whispers a barely audible "Thank you" as we bend down to kiss her goodbye and reluctantly leave the modest home.

Alice, an 80 year-old widow who got on a bus in New York and came to Atmore because she heard they needed help, and she wanted to see if she could do something. Could she ever!

She put us all to shame, helping cook and serve meals, mopping floors, doing dishes, cleaning bathrooms, and keeping everyone in line. She threatened every day to get on a bus and go on to Pensacola--but she was still there when I left.

Brandy, a nurse from Nashville, who "backed into" (her words) the position of chaplain for the working crew as well as the townspeople. One of the sweetest persons I could ever hope to meet.

Each evening, after supper, she carries out what she calls her "mission", massaging feet. Her strong soft fingers ease the pain of tired feet as she makes a personal connection with each one there. Many are shy about baring their feet, but very few turn her down after she quotes from Romans 10:15. "How beautiful are the feet of them that preach the gospel of peace, and bring glad tidings of good things."

As Brandy soothes tired feet, she also soothes tired aching souls with soft words of encouragement. She is the embodiment of a "personal touch".

Bill and Sue (not their real names). As I am driving through the county taking pictures of some of the damage, I spot a bearded middle-aged man sitting on the porch of a little country store. I strike up a conversation as I snap some photos of the surrounding destruction.

Part of the tin roof is off the store, and a neighbor is helping to board up a door where someone broke in last night and stole most of the undamaged merchandise. The bars on the windows and front door testify to the fact that this has been a common occurrence--common enough that they no longer have insurance.

Sue joins us on the porch and explains that because Bill has fibromylagia and pneumonia he no longer can do any of the work and they don't know if they can hang on any longer.

Their 16 year-old son has worked and saved for years to build an auto body shop. He recently erected a 20' x 40' pole barn behind the store and stocked it with the tools of the trade, ready to open his own business in a couple of weeks.

It is no longer there. Most of it is in a mangled pile among the trees on the other side of the road. During the storm someone helped themselves to most of the tools. No insurance there, either. Today the boy is down the road helping a neighbor repair his roof.

Yet these two people are praising God that no one was hurt, that none of their four children has ever been in trouble with the law or used drugs, and their youngest daughter, a straight-A student, was just chosen as a student ambassador to Australia.

Ivan has destroyed their property, but their spirit is very much alive, and they will survive.

SYMBOL OF HOPE

The winds have come, the winds have gone,
They did their very best
To tear apart this little town--
Put people to the test.

I walk around with broken heart
Amid destruction vast,
And, looking up, I spy a tree
I very nearly passed.

The little tree stands there alone
The branches bent and worn--
Reminds me of the town around
All broken and forlorn.

I study it with tear-filled eyes
And suddenly I see
A hundred buds of pink, I think,
Upon that little tree.

I study it again, and still
I can't believe my eyes.
Yes, there they are, on every branch,
Against the autumn skies.

I drive around the town and see
Destruction everywhere,
And yet there's life, and people come
To work and pray and share.

A few more days and I return.
The tree still draws me near,
For there it stands in glorious bloom--
A promise, "Do not fear!"

Impossible! I've never seen
Magnolias bloom in fall.
He's telling us He's still in charge.
There's hope yet for us all.

Reluctantly I leave behind
This symbol of God's love.
Though storms may come there still is life--
He's watching from above.

MY NOTES AND THOUGHTS

MY NOTES AND THOUGHTS

A WORD FROM ON HIGH

Most of these poems came from snippets of sermons. I always take notes when listening to a sermon, underlining ideas that I want to review later. A big asterisk calls my attention to an idea for a poem or short essay.

WHAT I DESERVE: Think about it. Do you really want to get everything that you deserve? A look at it from God's point of view.

DARK VALLEYS: A few extra thoughts on the phrase, "Yea, though I walk through the valley of the shadow……"

BITTER OR BETTER?: One of our pastor's favorite phrases. It is not what happens to us that determines our life, but how we react to those situations.

GOD'S GLUE: When life seems hopeless and everything is falling apart, God can put it back together again if we just allow him.

GOD'S PLEA: God speaks directly to us, begging us to share the good news of the Gospel with those around us.

DARK SHADOWS: When things look the darkest, that's when we need to turn toward the sun (Son).

I FORGOT: God always keeps His promises--unlike some of us--even when we have the best of intentions.

POSSIBILITIES: The thoughts in this poem came from the theme of a Christian Women's Conference which I attended in Gatlinburg, Tennessee

WHAT I DESERVE

"I didn't get what I deserved,"
I moaned with weeping eyes.
"I worked so hard to see it through,
But never won the prize."

"No matter what I try to do,
Someone will bring me down.
I try again, and still I fail
To gain the winner's crown."

"I work for God; I do His will
The best that I can see.
I search His word for truth and light;
But what's in it for me?"

(And God said)

"What you deserve! Child, are you sure
That is your heart's desire?
Your selfish thoughts and attitudes
Deserve a funeral pyre!"

"Did Christ deserve the rugged cross--
The hate of those He served?
Give thanks each day that you don't get
Just what you do deserve!"

DARK VALLEYS

Someday you may walk a dark valley;
Your life full of trouble and pain.
Don't worry--your Shepherd is with you
In days filled with sunshine or rain.

Rain falls on both righteous and sinner.
Tomorrow will be a new day.
Don't ask "Why me?", but "Why not me?",
A purpose you'll find on the way.

Just know as you walk through the valley
One day you will reach the far end.
With Jesus, your Shepherd, to lead you,
You'll rest in the arms of a friend.

BITTER OR BETTER?

When the troubles of lifetime assail you,
Experience teaching you well,
And the postman delivers
That old "Dear John" letter--
Is it making you bitter or better?

When you've practiced to sing with the choir
As soloist for the first time,
On the day of the concert
You can't find a sitter--
Does your world become better or bitter?

When the children are driving you crazy,
And the weather is keeping them in.
The baby needs changing--
The dog's even wetter--
Does it all make you bitter or better?

When you've worked your way up in the office
And the company "down-sizes" you,
Or a raging tornado
Leaves your home naught but litter--
Do you become better or bitter?

It is not what is going on 'round you
That determines the flow of your life--
It's the way you react--
Be a fighter or quitter--
And you will be better or bitter.

GOD'S GLUE

I came to God with broken heart--
A life all torn and tattered.
Decisions I had made in haste
Had left my ego shattered.

Satan whispered in my ear,
"There's nothing you can do.
You're too far down, there's no way out,
And God's abandoned you."

"He can't use you in His plan.
You might as well give up--
Not good enough to see His face,
Or at His table sup."

But still I prayed, and God reached down,
Picked up the broken shards,
Glued them together with His love,
Tied with forgiving cords.

And now my life is whole again.
God's glue holds it together.
His forgiveness and His love
Will hold in stormy weather.

GOD'S PLEA

I pled with you to ask your neighbor,
I begged you time and time again.
I asked you nothing but your labor
To harvest from the field of sin.

Don't you know that you offend me
With lack of action on your part?
I'm longing for the souls you'll send me;
Their suff'fing cuts me to the heart.

How will they know if you don't tell them?
How will they hear of Jesus' pain?
Of how He hung on Calvary's tree limb
And in a lonely cave was lain?

They won't know about His vict'ry
That over death--the battle won.
They'll never see the lights of Glory,
If you don't tell them 'bout my Son.

They need to learn about His caring.
Don't be so selfish with my love.
Go speak the words of truth with daring.
And I will bless you from above.

DARK SHADOWS

Dark shadows will come in all of our lives,
Remember they're not truly real.
They look so much bigger from where we observe
Compounded by fears that we feel.

A shadow can't hurt you, so don't be afraid:
They're changing, they come and they go.
There wouldn't be shadows without lots of light
Reflecting the ebb and the flow.

So turn toward the Son, look forward--not back;
And shadows you'll leave far behind.
With Jesus to guide you the shadows will flee
Like clouds, they will be silver lined.

I FORGOT

My mother said, "Go make your bed."
I promised that I would,
And then I went outside to play,
Not doing what I should--
Got all involved in other things--
Came in all flushed and hot.
When Mother asked, I just replied,
"I'm sorry, I forgot."

My neighbor called the other day
To ask me if I might
Make sure her windows all were closed
'Till she got home that night.
But I got busy with my own--
It really rained a lot--
And when she saw her soggy home
I just said, "I forgot."

Last night I dreamed that I had died
And stood at Heaven's gate.
The Book of Life was open wide.
Just what would be my fate?
I thought of all the things I'd done--
I knew I'd sinned a lot.
I bowed my head and asked for grace.
And God said, "I forgot."

POSSIBILITIES

I look out across the mountains
And imagine what could be
If I only truly followed
Every word He gives to me.

Imagination guides the future;
Opens possibilities;
Gives us eyes to see the heavens
And across the seven seas,

To a world as God intended
Full of living, caring souls
Looking up to praise the Father;
Striving on to holy goals.

Lord, I want to be a vessel
You can use to fill your plan.
Help me find and use my talents
As I serve my fellow man.

Help me grasp the higher vision,
Seizing opportunity,
Using my imagination;
Being all that I can be.

My Notes and Thoughts

DO UNTO OTHERS

Our Christianity means absolutely nothing if we are not living what we believe. We know we cannot be "good enough" to earn our way into Heaven. But our lives should reflect God's love to the world.

IN HIS PLACE: We truly are the only picture of God that many people will ever see.

THE SMILE: Even more contagious than the flu--and a lot more pleasant--is a smile. Pass it on!

THE HARVEST: Jesus has said, "Truly the fields are white to harvest, but the laborers are few." We are the laborers.

THE JESUS WAY: Sometimes we try so hard to do something for God. Then, if it doesn't work out, we wonder why. We forget to ask first what God wants.

GOD'S GARDEN: God can only use us if we are receptive. We have to get our pride out of the way before we can hear what He has to say.

HEEDING VS. HEARING: There's a lot of difference between what we hear and what we think we hear. Anyone who has been married knows that. We need to listen to God and then act upon what we have heard.

WAGGING TONGUES: Oh, how we love to hear gossip! And how tempting it is to pass on those little tidbits. But is it really the way we want to treat others?

LOOKING AND SEEING: Every day we walk by people with needs: a helping hand, an encouraging word, a pat on the back, a hug. We look at them but don't see the person inside.

LEAVING A LEGACY: Each of us would like to know that we will be remembered when we are gone. How we are remembered will depend on how we live our lives now.

IN HIS PLACE

(GOD'S AGENTS)

We're in the world in Jesus' place,
We are His hands and feet.
The image of our Savior's face
To everyone we meet.

We represent Him to the world,
We are His feet and hands.
It is through us His work is done
Both here and other lands.

A gentle word, a kindly smile,
Unselfish gifts of love,
The works we do reflect our faith
And point to God above.

So pray to God to help us be
His agents on this earth.
Control our thoughts and curb our tongues
And praise our Savior's birth.

And as we go about our life
Remember we might be
The only photograph of Him
That some will ever see.

THE SMILE

I saw a smiling face today
And my heart jumped with glee,
Because that smile was found upon
A face that looked at me

Deep down inside my sinful heart
The happiness did well
Because it knew the reason why,
And could the story tell,

Of someone who had lent a hand
Upon life's burdened way
To someone else who felt the burden
Weigh him down that day.

Yes, I can laugh and I can sing,
And I, too wear a smile
Because it was my sin-stained hand
That helped another smile.

THE HARVEST

You can't take part in the harvest
If you never get out in the field.
You won't see God in His kingdom
If your heart is too hardened to yield.

A worker who's willing to serve Him
Won't care what assignment He gives.
He'll labor his best in the vineyard
By witnessing right where he lives.

No matter your wisdom or talent,
No matter your shape or your size,
God uses the soul that is willing
To harvest more souls to the skies.

Don't be a respecter of status,
Don't worry 'bout color or means,
For the souls that are missed in the harvest
The Devil will come in and glean.

THE JESUS WAY

Stand up for what is right and just
'Tho others say you're wrong.
Take up your cross and follow Him
And sing His joyful song.

Look up to Jesus for your strength.
Don't dwell on failures past.
No sorrow, pity--look for peace--
He'll give you power vast.

Grow up--get off the baby's milk.
Don't stagnate where you are.
You'll blow up if you're immature.
His knowledge takes you far.

So read His Word--digest the meat
No matter what they say.
The difference is in your response.
Just walk the Jesus way.

GOD'S GARDEN

A farmer goes to plant his field
But 'ere he sows the seeds
He must prepare hardscrabble earth--
Cut down the thorns and weeds,

Then work the soil with plow or hoe--
Break down the hardened sod,
Remove the rocks and tangled roots,
And pulverize the clods.

And so God works upon our lives
To cultivate within--
The rocks of stubbornness and pride--
The roots of filthy sin.

He breaks us down to build us up.
We ne'er can be of use
As long as we cannot be tilled
His garden won't produce.

So in our heart he sows His seed
And waters it with love,
And then our meek receptive soul
Reflects our Lord above.

HEEDING vs. HEARING

You sat in church this morning
And listened to God's word
Then out the door you sauntered--
Forgetting what you heard.

I know you've read your Bible,
But, neighbor, do you heed
And try to follow Jesus
In thought and word and deed?

Sometimes we make excuses
Or just misunderstand--
Our loving Lord expects us
To lend a helping hand.

Or are we just too busy
To listen or to heed?
We're not to be indifferent--
Ignoring those in need.

With thoughtful contemplation;
With heart as well as ear;
We need determined action
To heed the things we hear.

WAGGING TONGUES

(Proverbs 26:17-28)

Gossip is a fuel
That feeds destructive fires.
The tongue can do more damage
Than any funeral pyre.

A tale that's passed among you
Destroys a person's life,
Or tears apart a church group
By causing pain and strife.

Don't feed those fiery embers
About a friend or foe.
Ask God to help you quench them--
Let them no farther go.

Ignore those juicy secrets--
They're better left unknown.
Someday that open closet
May be your very own.

And all that dirty linen
That you have hid so well
May become the gossip
For someone else to tell.

LOOKING AND SEEING

When Jesus walked upon this earth
He saw with knowing eyes.
The hurt, the lame, the ill and blind
Were healed as He passed by.

Every day along our way
We look at those around,
But we don't see what's really there:
The hurt will ne'er be found.

Unless we look with godly eyes
That search beneath the skin,
We'll never know the pain and strife;
The agony within.

The blind can't see the green, green grass
Or rainbows in the skies;
And we can't see the love of God
Without salvation's eyes.

And when we look and really see,
We'll know what needs are there.
And then, like Jesus, we'll respond
To show how much we care.

LEAVING A LEGACY

I wonder what I'll leave behind
When Jesus calls me home.
Will anyone remember me--
That on the earth I roamed?

It's really not important
That someone knows my name
From articles in magazines
'Bout wisdom, wealth, or fame.

No matter if my walls are filled
With trophies or awards--
But did I speak with those I met
And tell them of my Lord?

And did my children see in me
The love of God on high?
Was my example good enough
To point them to the sky?

Did I live out the Golden Rule
In work and business deals?
Can people count on me to help
No matter how I feel?

The fickle winds will soon destroy
Our footprints on this earth.
Our actions as we tread the way
Determine what we're worth.

I pray that God will use me up
'Til there's no more of me,
And service to my fellow man
Will be my legacy.

MY NOTES AND THOUGHTS

MY NOTES AND THOUGHTS

ABOUT THE AUTHOR

Dorothy Skinner Dale was born in 1938 in South Haven, Michigan and raised on a farm near there. She attended a one-room school, and taught at another one-room school after graduating from Hope College in Holland, Michigan. She moved to Tennessee in 1989 after the death of her late husband, Richard. She has one son, Daniel, who still lives in Michigan, and several step-children. Her husband, Willard, is a pastor.

Mrs. Dale started writing poetry in her mid-teens. She has many interests including knitting, crocheting, singing, various crafts, and going on mission construction trips. She volunteers at Habitat for Humanity and is the song leader at her church.